ARCHABET

An Architectural Alphabet   Photographs by Balthazar Korab

GW00505580

National Trust for Historic Preservation

T H E   P R E S E R V A T I O N   P R E S S

The Preservation Press
National Trust for Historic Preservation
1785 Massachusetts Avenue, N.W.
Washington, D.C. 20036

The National Trust for Historic Preservation in the United States is the only private, nonprofit national organization chartered by Congress to encourage public participation in the preservation of sites, buildings, and objects significant in American history and culture. Support is provided by membership dues, endowment funds, contributions, and grants from federal agencies, including the U.S. Department of the Interior, under provisions of the National Historic Preservation Act of 1966. For information about membership in the National Trust, write to Membership at the above address.

ARCHABET, the book on which this collection of postcards is based, was first developed and edited by Diane Maddex.

Designed by Marc Alain Meadows and Robert Wiser, Meadows & Wiser, Washington, D.C.

The postcards in this book are oversized and require letter-rate postage.

Printed in South Korea by Sung In

96 95 94 93 92   5 4 3 2 1

ISBN 0-89133-192-1

P R E F A C E

Under huge chestnut trees, in a formidable brick school, I learned my ABCs from a teacher who carved letters on the blackboard with squeaky chalk. Long on the road since then, I have met other symbols from other worlds: elegant white characters on a 15-story red scroll on my Shanghai hotel, tiny wedge-shaped Sumerian cuneiforms, arabesques caked with whitewash on mosques in Yemen—all with messages, but not for me. S.P.Q.R. inscribed in the streets of Rome, illuminated manuscripts, Rimbaud's colored poetry—these still hold the most magic for me and are the alphabets of my world. When converted to musical notation, letters are charged with even richer emotional content. Indeed, the basic purpose of the letter is to convert sound, whether speech or the link between us and music of another kind: the frozen music, architecture.

Balthazar Korab

Learning to look is a pleasure;
the buildings will embrace your eyes.

Judith Lynch Waldhorn

Gothic Revival house, Romeo, Michigan

FROM *ARCHABET: AN ARCHITECTURAL ALPHABET*, PUBLISHED BY THE PRESERVATION PRESS, NATIONAL TRUST FOR HISTORIC PRESERVATION • 1992 BALTHAZAR KORAB, QUOTATION FROM *A GIFT TO THE STREET* BY CAROL OLWELL AND JUDITH LYNCH WALDHORN, 1976, REPRINT NEW YORK, ST. MARTIN'S PRESS, 1983.

Architecture begins where engineering ends.

WALTER GROPIUS

FROM *ARCHART: AN ARCHITECTURAL ALPHABET*, PUBLISHED BY THE PRESERVATION PRESS, NATIONAL TRUST FOR HISTORIC PRESERVATION. © 1992 BALTHAZAR KORAB. QUOTATION FROM A SPEECH BY WALTER GROPIUS, 1938. *SEE ARCHITECTURE IN AMERICA* BY PAUL HEYER, 1966. REVISED. NEW DIRECTIONS IN AMERICAN ARCHITECTURE. NEW YORK: WALKER, 1978.

B

*Sherman Minton Bridge over the Ohio River
between Louisville, Kentucky, and New Albany, Indiana*

It is not enough to see architecture; you must experience it.

STEEN EILER RASMUSSEN

C

Interior of the cupola at Longwood
Natchez, Mississippi

The art of building, or architecture, is the beginning of all the arts that lie outside the person.

HAVELOCK ELLIS

PHOTO © 1992 BALTHAZAR KORAB, FROM *ARCHABET: AN ARCHITECTURAL ALPHABET*, PUBLISHED BY THE PRESERVATION PRESS, NATIONAL TRUST FOR HISTORIC PRESERVATION. © 1992 BALTHAZAR KORAB. QUOTATION FROM *THE DANCE OF LIFE* BY HAVELOCK ELLIS, 1923; REPRINT WESTPORT, CONN., GREENWOOD PRESS, 1973.

D

Good Luck gas station, Dallas, Texas

Architecture, simply and immediately perceived,
is a combination, revealed through light and shade, of spaces,
of masses, and of lines.

GEOFFREY SCOTT

E

Split rail fence at Meffords Fort
Washington, Kentucky

Architecture can reach out beyond the period of its birth, beyond the social class that called it into being, beyond the style to which it belongs.

Sigfried Giedion

F

Sawn-wood porch, Monroe, Michigan

FROM *ARCHABET: AN ARCHITECTURAL ALPHABET* PUBLISHED BY THE PRESERVATION PRESS, NATIONAL TRUST FOR HISTORIC PRESERVATION; © 1992 BALTHAZAR KORAB. QUOTATION FROM *SPACE, TIME AND ARCHITECTURE: THE GROWTH OF A NEW TRADITION*, BY SIGFRIED GIEDION, CAMBRIDGE, MASS., HARVARD UNIVERSITY PRESS, 1941.

All styles are good except the boring kind.

VOLTAIRE

G

Honolulu House, Marshall, Michigan

Well-building hath three conditions:
Commodity, Firmness, and Delight.

Sir Henry Wotton

FROM *ARCHARET AN ARCHITECTURAL ALPHABET* PUBLISHED BY THE PRESERVATION PRESS, NATIONAL TRUST FOR HISTORIC PRESERVATION. © 1992 BALTHAZAR KORAB. QUOTATION AFTER VITRUVIUS IN *THE TEN BOOKS ON ARCHITECTURE* BOOK 1, CHAPTER III, FROM *THE ELEMENTS OF ARCHITECTURE* BY SIR HENRY WOTTON, 1624. REPRINT NORWOOD, N.J.: WALTER J. JOHNSON, 1970.

H

Stanton Hall, Natchez, Mississippi

Ornament if organic was never *on* the thing but *of* it....

FRANK LLOYD WRIGHT

I

Silos on a farm, Monroe, Michigan

FROM *ARCHABET, AN ARCHITECTURAL ALPHABET* PUBLISHED BY THE PRESERVATION PRESS, NATIONAL TRUST FOR HISTORIC PRESERVATION © 1992 BALTHAZAR KORAB. QUOTATION FROM *A TESTAMENT*, BY FRANK LLOYD WRIGHT, NEW YORK, HORIZON PRESS, 1957.

God is in the detail.

LUDWIG MIES VAN DER ROHE

J

Huntington House, Howell, Michigan

FROM *ARCHABET: AN ARCHITECTURAL ALPHABET* PUBLISHED BY THE PRESERVATION PRESS, NATIONAL TRUST FOR HISTORIC PRESERVATION. © 1992 BALTHAZAR KORAB. QUOTATION WAS THE PERSONAL MOTTO OF LUDWIG MIES VAN DER ROHE. SEE "MIES VAN DER ROHE" BY LUDWIG GLAESER. IN *MACMILLAN ENCYCLOPEDIA OF ARCHITECTS*, VOL. 3. EDITED BY ADOLF K. PLACZEK. NEW YORK: FREE PRESS, MACMILLAN, 1982.

Form ever follows function.

Louis Henri Sullivan

K

Abandoned gravel pit, Oxford, Michigan

All architecture is shelter; all great architecture is the design
of space that contains, cuddles, exalts, or stimulates the persons
in that space.

PHILIP JOHNSON

L

Elms Court, Natchez, Mississippi

FROM *ARCHABET: AN ARCHITECTURAL ALPHABET*, PUBLISHED BY THE PRESERVATION PRESS, NATIONAL TRUST FOR HISTORIC PRESERVATION. © 1992 BALTHAZAR KORAB. QUOTATION FROM
"WHAT MAKES ME TICK," SPEECH BY PHILIP JOHNSON, COLUMBIA UNIVERSITY, 1975. IN *PHILIP JOHNSON: WRITINGS*, NEW YORK: OXFORD UNIVERSITY PRESS, 1979.

Consider... the momentous event in architecture when the wall parted and the column became.

Louis I. Kahn

Rotunda of the Minnesota State Capitol
St. Paul, Minnesota

We shape our buildings, and afterwards our buildings shape us.

WINSTON S. CHURCHILL

N

Half-timbered house
Old Salem, North Carolina

FROM *ARCHABET: AN ARCHITECTURAL ALPHABET*, PUBLISHED BY THE PRESERVATION PRESS, NATIONAL TRUST FOR HISTORIC PRESERVATION. © 1992 BALTHAZAR KORAB. QUOTATION FROM SPEECH BY WINSTON S. CHURCHILL, OCTOBER 28, 1943. SEE *WINSTON S. CHURCHILL: HIS COMPLETE SPEECHES, 1897–1963*, EDITED BY ROBERT RHODES JAMES, NEW YORK, CHELSEA HOUSE, 1974.

Form is not the aim of our work, but only the result.
Form, by itself, does not exist.

LUDWIG MIES VAN DER ROHE

Gate near the Mississippi River in Louisiana

When we build, let us think that we build for ever.

JOHN RUSKIN

P

Lamp post at the Kingswood School
Bloomfield Hills, Michigan

FROM *ARCHABET: AN ARCHITECTURAL ALPHABET*, PUBLISHED BY THE PRESERVATION PRESS, NATIONAL TRUST FOR HISTORIC PRESERVATION. © 1992 BALTHAZAR KORAB. QUOTATION FROM *THE SEVEN LAMPS OF ARCHITECTURE*, BY JOHN RUSKIN, 1849. REPRINT NEW YORK: FARRAR, STRAUS AND GIROUX, 1961.

Less is more.

Ludwig Mies van der Rohe

Q

Windmill near a farmhouse
Fenton, Michigan

FROM *ARCHART: AN ARCHITECTURAL ALPHABET* PUBLISHED BY THE PRESERVATION PRESS, NATIONAL TRUST FOR HISTORIC PRESERVATION © 1992 BALTHAZAR KORAB. QUOTATION IS PERSONAL MOTTO OF LUDWIG MIES VAN DER ROHE. SEE *MIES VAN DER ROHE* BY PHILIP JOHNSON, 1947. NEW YORK: MUSEUM OF MODERN ART, 1978.

I like complexity and contradiction in architecture. . . .
I am for messy vitality over obvious unity. . . . I am for richness
of meaning rather than clarity of meaning; for the implicit
function as well as the explicit function.

Robert Venturi

R

Sawyer House, Monroe, Michigan

I call architecture frozen music.

JOHANN WOLFGANG VON GOETHE

S

Balcony grillwork in the Vieux Carré
New Orleans, Louisiana

FROM *ARCHABET: AN ARCHITECTURAL ALPHABET* PUBLISHED BY THE PRESERVATION PRESS, NATIONAL TRUST FOR HISTORIC PRESERVATION. © 1992 BALTHAZAR KORAB. QUOTATION IN LETTER FROM GOETHE TO ECKERMANN, FEBRUARY 4, 1829.

Architecture is the masterly, correct and magnificent play
of volumes brought together in light.

Le Corbusier

T

Entrance portico of the Cranbrook Art Academy
Bloomfield Hills, Michigan

FROM *ARCHABET, AN ARCHITECTURAL ALPHABET.* PUBLISHED BY THE PRESERVATION PRESS, NATIONAL TRUST FOR HISTORIC PRESERVATION. © 1992 BALTHAZAR KORAB. QUOTATION FROM *VERS UNE ARCHITECTURE,* BY LE CORBUSIER. 1922. PARIS: ARTHAUD. 1977.

Architecture, like music, must be a part of the composer, but it must also transcend him to give something to music or architecture itself. Mozart is not only Mozart, but music.

LOUIS I. KAHN

Porch of the Tampa Bay Hotel
Tampa, Florida

FROM *ARCHABET: AN ARCHITECTURAL ALPHABET* PUBLISHED BY THE PRESERVATION PRESS, NATIONAL TRUST FOR HISTORIC PRESERVATION. © 1992 BALTHAZAR KORAB. QUOTATION FROM *BETWEEN SILENCE AND LIGHT: SPIRIT IN THE ARCHITECTURE OF LOUIS I. KAHN* BY JOHN LOBELL. BOULDER, COLO.: SHAMBHALA PUBLICATIONS, 1979.

We may live without her [architecture], and worship without
her, but we cannot remember without her.

JOHN RUSKIN

V

Old brick paving, Savannah, Georgia

One of modern architecture's greatest failings has been its
lack of interest in the relationship of the building to the sky.
One doubts that a poem was ever written to a flat-roofed
building silhouetted against the setting sun.

PAUL RUDOLPH

W

Chapel of the Air Force Academy
Colorado Springs, Colorado

FROM *ARCHITECT: AN ARCHITECTURAL ALPHABET*, PUBLISHED BY THE PRESERVATION PRESS/NATIONAL TRUST FOR HISTORIC PRESERVATIONS © 1992 RAUTHACAR KORAB. QUOTATIONS FROM PAUL RUDOLPH, "ON ARCHITECTURAL *ARCHITECTURE IN AMERICA* BY PAUL HEYER, 1966. REV. ED. NEW YORK: WALKER, 1978.

Architecture occurs when a building and a person like each other.

WILLIAM WAYNE CAUDILL, WILLIAM MERRIWEATHER PENA, AND PAUL KENNON

Door of a house, Monroe, Michigan

FROM *ARCHIABET: AN ARCHITECTURAL ALPHABET* PUBLISHED BY THE PRESERVATION PRESS, NATIONAL TRUST FOR HISTORIC PRESERVATION © 1992 BALTHAZAR KORAB

QUOTATION FROM *ARCHITECTURE AND YOU: HOW TO EXPERIENCE AND ENJOY BUILDINGS* BY WILLIAM WAYNE CAUDILL, WILLIAM MERRIWEATHER PENA, AND PAUL KENNON, NEW YORK:

WHITNEY LIBRARY OF DESIGN, 1978.

Architecture, unlike other arts, is not an escape from, but an acceptance of, the human condition, including its many frailties as well as the technical advances of its scientists and engineers.

PIETRO BELLUSCHI

Gothic Revival house, Washington, Kentucky

Let us, while waiting for new monuments, preserve the ancient monuments.

Victor Hugo

Z

Cast-iron stairway in the City Hall
Bay City, Michigan

FROM *ARCHABET: AN ARCHITECTURAL ALPHABET*. PUBLISHED BY THE PRESERVATION PRESS, NATIONAL TRUST FOR HISTORIC PRESERVATION. © 1992 BALTHAZAR KORAB. QUOTATION FROM 1832.